QUARTER BOUND PRESS

2014 WEEKLY PLANNER

Quarter Bound Press
A Library of Congress Approved Publisher
www.QuarterBoundPress.com

www.quarterboundpress.com/datebook.html
Book design by Karen Izbinski

Quarter Bound Press and colophon are registered trademarks of Quarter Bound Press. Contact the publisher for information regarding publishing and special discounts on bulk purchases at serivces@quarterboundpress.com.

ISBN-10: 0-9830211-2-0 EAN-13: 978-0-9830211-2-4

Printed in the United States of America
10 9 8 7 6 5 4 3 2 1

QUARTER BOUND PRESS

2014 WEEKLY PLANNER

Thank you for choosing this Quarter Bound Press product. The only thing that could make this a better planner is if there were more hours in a day. Quarter Bound Press is committed to developing products that keep your life organized.

Be kind.
Be polite.
Think positively.
Act responsibly.
Say, "Please" and "Thank You".
Care about other people's feelings.
Do a good deed for the day to feel good.

Quarter Bound Press Office Products
quarterboundpress.com

Made in U.S.A.
Res Non Verba.

January 2013

	Sun	Mon	Tue	Wed	Thu	Fri	Sat
1			1	2	3	4	5
2	6	7	8	9	10	11	12
3	13	14	15	16	17	18	19
4	20	21	22	23	24	25	26
5	27	28	29	30	31		

February 2013

	Sun	Mon	Tue	Wed	Thu	Fri	Sat
5						1	2
6	3	4	5	6	7	8	9
7	10	11	12	13	14	15	16
8	17	18	19	20	21	22	23
9	24	25	26	27	28		

March 2013

	Sun	Mon	Tue	Wed	Thu	Fri	Sat
9						1	2
10	3	4	5	6	7	8	9
11	10	11	12	13	14	15	16
12	17	18	19	20	21	22	23
13	24	25	26	27	28	29	30
14	31						

April 2013

	Sun	Mon	Tue	Wed	Thu	Fri	Sat
14		1	2	3	4	5	6
15	7	8	9	10	11	12	13
16	14	15	16	17	18	19	20
17	21	22	23	24	25	26	27
18	28	29	30				

May 2013

	Sun	Mon	Tue	Wed	Thu	Fri	Sat
18				1	2	3	4
19	5	6	7	8	9	10	11
20	12	13	14	15	16	17	18
21	19	20	21	22	23	24	25
22	26	27	28	29	30	31	

June 2013

	Sun	Mon	Tue	Wed	Thu	Fri	Sat
22							1
23	2	3	4	5	6	7	8
24	9	10	11	12	13	14	15
25	16	17	18	19	20	21	22
26	23	24	25	26	27	28	29
27	30						

July 2013

	Sun	Mon	Tue	Wed	Thu	Fri	Sat
27		1	2	3	4	5	6
28	7	8	9	10	11	12	13
29	14	15	16	17	18	19	20
30	21	22	23	24	25	26	27
31	28	29	30	31			

August 2013

	Sun	Mon	Tue	Wed	Thu	Fri	Sat
31					1	2	3
32	4	5	6	7	8	9	10
33	11	12	13	14	15	16	17
34	18	19	20	21	22	23	24
35	25	26	27	28	29	30	31

September 2013

	Sun	Mon	Tue	Wed	Thu	Fri	Sat
36	1	2	3	4	5	6	7
37	8	9	10	11	12	13	14
38	15	16	17	18	19	20	21
39	22	23	24	25	26	27	28
40	29	30					

October 2013

	Sun	Mon	Tue	Wed	Thu	Fri	Sat
40			1	2	3	4	5
41	6	7	8	9	10	11	12
42	13	14	15	16	17	18	19
43	20	21	22	23	24	25	26
44	27	28	29	30	31		

November 2013

	Sun	Mon	Tue	Wed	Thu	Fri	Sat
44						1	2
45	3	4	5	6	7	8	9
46	10	11	12	13	14	15	16
47	17	18	19	20	21	22	23
48	24	25	26	27	28	29	30

December 2013

	Sun	Mon	Tue	Wed	Thu	Fri	Sat
49	1	2	3	4	5	6	7
50	8	9	10	11	12	13	14
51	15	16	17	18	19	20	21
52	22	23	24	25	26	27	28
1	29	30	31				

January 2014

	Sun	Mon	Tue	Wed	Thu	Fri	Sat
1				1	2	3	4
2	5	6	7	8	9	10	11
3	12	13	14	15	16	17	18
4	19	20	21	22	23	24	25
5	26	27	28	29	30	31	

February 2014

	Sun	Mon	Tue	Wed	Thu	Fri	Sat
5							1
6	2	3	4	5	6	7	8
7	9	10	11	12	13	14	15
8	16	17	18	19	20	21	22
9	23	24	25	26	27	28	

March 2014

	Sun	Mon	Tue	Wed	Thu	Fri	Sat
9							1
10	2	3	4	5	6	7	8
11	9	10	11	12	13	14	15
12	16	17	18	19	20	21	22
13	23	24	25	26	27	28	29
14	30	31					

April 2014

	Sun	Mon	Tue	Wed	Thu	Fri	Sat
14			1	2	3	4	5
15	6	7	8	9	10	11	12
16	13	14	15	16	17	18	19
17	20	21	22	23	24	25	26
18	27	28	29	30			

May 2014

	Sun	Mon	Tue	Wed	Thu	Fri	Sat
18					1	2	3
19	4	5	6	7	8	9	10
20	11	12	13	14	15	16	17
21	18	19	20	21	22	23	24
22	25	26	27	28	29	30	31

June 2014

	Sun	Mon	Tue	Wed	Thu	Fri	Sat
23	1	2	3	4	5	6	7
24	8	9	10	11	12	13	14
25	15	16	17	18	19	20	21
26	22	23	24	25	26	27	28
27	29	30					

July 2014

	Sun	Mon	Tue	Wed	Thu	Fri	Sat
27			1	2	3	4	5
28	6	7	8	9	10	11	12
29	13	14	15	16	17	18	19
30	20	21	22	23	24	25	26
31	27	28	29	30	31		

August 2014

	Sun	Mon	Tue	Wed	Thu	Fri	Sat
31						1	2
32	3	4	5	6	7	8	9
33	10	11	12	13	14	15	16
34	17	18	19	20	21	22	23
35	24	25	26	27	28	29	30
36	31						

September 2014

	Sun	Mon	Tue	Wed	Thu	Fri	Sat
36		1	2	3	4	5	6
37	7	8	9	10	11	12	13
38	14	15	16	17	18	19	20
39	21	22	23	24	25	26	27
40	28	29	30				

October 2014

	Sun	Mon	Tue	Wed	Thu	Fri	Sat
40				1	2	3	4
41	5	6	7	8	9	10	11
42	12	13	14	15	16	17	18
43	19	20	21	22	23	24	25
44	26	27	28	29	30	31	

November 2014

	Sun	Mon	Tue	Wed	Thu	Fri	Sat
44							1
45	2	3	4	5	6	7	8
46	9	10	11	12	13	14	15
47	16	17	18	19	20	21	22
48	23	24	25	26	27	28	29
49	30						

December 2014

	Sun	Mon	Tue	Wed	Thu	Fri	Sat
49		1	2	3	4	5	6
50	7	8	9	10	11	12	13
51	14	15	16	17	18	19	20
52	21	22	23	24	25	26	27
1	28	29	30	31			

January 2015

	Sun	Mon	Tue	Wed	Thu	Fri	Sat
1					1	2	3
2	4	5	6	7	8	9	10
3	11	12	13	14	15	16	17
4	18	19	20	21	22	23	24
5	25	26	27	28	29	30	31

February 2015

	Sun	Mon	Tue	Wed	Thu	Fri	Sat
6	1	2	3	4	5	6	7
7	8	9	10	11	12	13	14
8	15	16	17	18	19	20	21
9	22	23	24	25	26	27	28

March 2015

	Sun	Mon	Tue	Wed	Thu	Fri	Sat
10	1	2	3	4	5	6	7
11	8	9	10	11	12	13	14
12	15	16	17	18	19	20	21
13	22	23	24	25	26	27	28
14	29	30	31				

April 2015

	Sun	Mon	Tue	Wed	Thu	Fri	Sat
14				1	2	3	4
15	5	6	7	8	9	10	11
16	12	13	14	15	16	17	18
17	19	20	21	22	23	24	25
18	26	27	28	29	30		

May 2015

	Sun	Mon	Tue	Wed	Thu	Fri	Sat
18						1	2
19	3	4	5	6	7	8	9
20	10	11	12	13	14	15	16
21	17	18	19	20	21	22	23
22	24	25	26	27	28	29	30
23	31						

June 2015

	Sun	Mon	Tue	Wed	Thu	Fri	Sat
23		1	2	3	4	5	6
24	7	8	9	10	11	12	13
25	14	15	16	17	18	19	20
26	21	22	23	24	25	26	27
27	28	29	30				

July 2015

	Sun	Mon	Tue	Wed	Thu	Fri	Sat
27				1	2	3	4
28	5	6	7	8	9	10	11
29	12	13	14	15	16	17	18
30	19	20	21	22	23	24	25
31	26	27	28	29	30	31	

August 2015

	Sun	Mon	Tue	Wed	Thu	Fri	Sat
31							1
32	2	3	4	5	6	7	8
33	9	10	11	12	13	14	15
34	16	17	18	19	20	21	22
35	23	24	25	26	27	28	29
36	30	31					

September 2015

	Sun	Mon	Tue	Wed	Thu	Fri	Sat
36			1	2	3	4	5
37	6	7	8	9	10	11	12
38	13	14	15	16	17	18	19
39	20	21	22	23	24	25	26
40	27	28	29	30			

October 2015

	Sun	Mon	Tue	Wed	Thu	Fri	Sat
40					1	2	3
41	4	5	6	7	8	9	10
42	11	12	13	14	15	16	17
43	18	19	20	21	22	23	24
44	25	26	27	28	29	30	31

November 2015

	Sun	Mon	Tue	Wed	Thu	Fri	Sat
45	1	2	3	4	5	6	7
46	8	9	10	11	12	13	14
47	15	16	17	18	19	20	21
48	22	23	24	25	26	27	28
49	29	30					

December 2015

	Sun	Mon	Tue	Wed	Thu	Fri	Sat
49			1	2	3	4	5
50	6	7	8	9	10	11	12
51	13	14	15	16	17	18	19
52	20	21	22	23	24	25	26
1	27	28	29	30	31		

January 2016

	Sun	Mon	Tue	Wed	Thu	Fri	Sat
53						1	2
1	3	4	5	6	7	8	9
2	10	11	12	13	14	15	16
3	17	18	19	20	21	22	23
4	24	25	26	27	28	29	30
5	31						

February 2016

	Sun	Mon	Tue	Wed	Thu	Fri	Sat
5		1	2	3	4	5	6
6	7	8	9	10	11	12	13
7	14	15	16	17	18	19	20
8	21	22	23	24	25	26	27
9	28	29					

March 2016

	Sun	Mon	Tue	Wed	Thu	Fri	Sat
9			1	2	3	4	5
10	6	7	8	9	10	11	12
11	13	14	15	16	17	18	19
12	20	21	22	23	24	25	26
13	27	28	29	30	31		

April 2016

	Sun	Mon	Tue	Wed	Thu	Fri	Sat
13						1	2
14	3	4	5	6	7	8	9
15	10	11	12	13	14	15	16
16	17	18	19	20	21	22	23
17	24	25	26	27	28	29	30

May 2016

	Sun	Mon	Tue	Wed	Thu	Fri	Sat
18	1	2	3	4	5	6	7
19	8	9	10	11	12	13	14
20	15	16	17	18	19	20	21
21	22	23	24	25	26	27	28
22	29	30	31				

June 2016

	Sun	Mon	Tue	Wed	Thu	Fri	Sat
22				1	2	3	4
23	5	6	7	8	9	10	11
24	12	13	14	15	16	17	18
25	19	20	21	22	23	24	25
26	26	27	28	29	30		

July 2016

	Sun	Mon	Tue	Wed	Thu	Fri	Sat
26						1	2
27	3	4	5	6	7	8	9
28	10	11	12	13	14	15	16
29	17	18	19	20	21	22	23
30	24	25	26	27	28	29	30
31	31						

August 2016

	Sun	Mon	Tue	Wed	Thu	Fri	Sat
31		1	2	3	4	5	6
32	7	8	9	10	11	12	13
33	14	15	16	17	18	19	20
34	21	22	23	24	25	26	27
35	28	29	30	31			

September 2016

	Sun	Mon	Tue	Wed	Thu	Fri	Sat
35					1	2	3
36	4	5	6	7	8	9	10
37	11	12	13	14	15	16	17
38	18	19	20	21	22	23	24
39	25	26	27	28	29	30	

October 2016

	Sun	Mon	Tue	Wed	Thu	Fri	Sat
39							1
40	2	3	4	5	6	7	8
41	9	10	11	12	13	14	15
42	16	17	18	19	20	21	22
43	23	24	25	26	27	28	29
44	30	31					

November 2016

	Sun	Mon	Tue	Wed	Thu	Fri	Sat
44			1	2	3	4	5
45	6	7	8	9	10	11	12
46	13	14	15	16	17	18	19
47	20	21	22	23	24	25	26
48	27	28	29	30			

December 2016

	Sun	Mon	Tue	Wed	Thu	Fri	Sat
48					1	2	3
49	4	5	6	7	8	9	10
50	11	12	13	14	15	16	17
51	18	19	20	21	22	23	24
52	25	26	27	28	29	30	31

ANNIVERSARIES, BIRTHDAYS & OTHER SPECIAL DATES

MONTH	DAY	OCCASION

ANNIVERSARIES, BIRTHDAYS & OTHER SPECIAL DATES

MONTH	DAY	OCCASION

October 2013

MONDAY 28	TUESDAY 29	WEDNESDAY 30
8 AM	8 AM	8 AM
9	9	9
10	10	10
11	11	11
12 PM	12 PM	12 PM
1	1	1
2	2	2
3	3	3
4	4	4
5	5	5
6	6	6
7	7	7
8	8	8
9	9	9
10	10	10

November 2013

THURSDAY 31

8 AM
9
10
11
12 PM
1
2
3
4
5
6
7
8
9
10

FRIDAY 1

8 AM
9
10
11
12 PM
1
2
3
4
5
6
7
8
9
10

SATURDAY 2

8 AM
9
10
11
12 PM
1
2
3
4
5
6
7
8
9

SUNDAY 3

8 AM
9
10
11
12 PM
1
2
3
4
5
6
7
8
9

November 2013

MONDAY 4

8 AM

9

10

11

12 PM

1

2

3

4

5

6

7

8

9

10

TUESDAY 5

8 AM

9

10

11

12 PM

1

2

3

4

5

6

7

8

9

10

WEDNESDAY 6

8 AM

9

10

11

12 PM

1

2

3

4

5

6

7

8

9

10

THURSDAY 7

8 AM

9

10

11

12 PM

1

2

3

4

5

6

7

8

9

10

FRIDAY 8

8 AM

9

10

11

12 PM

1

2

3

4

5

6

7

8

9

10

SATURDAY 9

8 AM
9
10
11
12 PM
1
2
3
4
5
6
7
8
9

SUNDAY 10

8 AM
9
10
11
12 PM
1
2
3
4
5
6
7
8
9

November 2013

MONDAY 11

8 AM

9

10

11

12 PM

1

2

3

4

5

6

7

8

9

10

TUESDAY 12

8 AM

9

10

11

12 PM

1

2

3

4

5

6

7

8

9

10

WEDNESDAY 13

8 AM

9

10

11

12 PM

1

2

3

4

5

6

7

8

9

10

November 2013

THURSDAY 14

8 AM

9

10

11

12 PM

1

2

3

4

5

6

7

8

9

10

FRIDAY 15

8 AM

9

10

11

12 PM

1

2

3

4

5

6

7

8

9

10

SATURDAY 16

8 AM

9

10

11

12 PM

1

2

3

4

5

6

7

8

9

SUNDAY 17

8 AM

9

10

11

12 PM

1

2

3

4

5

6

7

8

9

November 2013

MONDAY 18	TUESDAY 19	WEDNESDAY 20
8 AM	8 AM	8 AM
9	9	9
10	10	10
11	11	11
12 PM	12 PM	12 PM
1	1	1
2	2	2
3	3	3
4	4	4
5	5	5
6	6	6
7	7	7
8	8	8
9	9	9
10	10	10

November 2013

THURSDAY 21

8 AM

9

10

11

12 PM

1

2

3

4

5

6

7

8

9

10

FRIDAY 22

8 AM

9

10

11

12 PM

1

2

3

4

5

6

7

8

9

10

SATURDAY 23

8 AM

9

10

11

12 PM

1

2

3

4

5

6

7

8

9

SUNDAY 24

8 AM

9

10

11

12 PM

1

2

3

4

5

6

7

8

9

November 2013

MONDAY 25

8 AM
9
10
11
12 PM
1
2
3
4
5
6
7
8
9
10

TUESDAY 26

8 AM
9
10
11
12 PM
1
2
3
4
5
6
7
8
9
10

WEDNESDAY 27

8 AM
9
10
11
12 PM
1
2
3
4
5
6
7
8
9
10

December 2013

THURSDAY 28

8 AM

9

10

11

12 PM

1

2

3

4

5

6

7

8

9

10

FRIDAY 29

8 AM

9

10

11

12 PM

1

2

3

4

5

6

7

8

9

10

SATURDAY 30

8 AM

9

10

11

12 PM

1

2

3

4

5

6

7

8

9

SUNDAY 1

8 AM

9

10

11

12 PM

1

2

3

4

5

6

7

8

9

December 2013

MONDAY 2

8 AM
9
10
11
12 PM
1
2
3
4
5
6
7
8
9
10

TUESDAY 3

8 AM
9
10
11
12 PM
1
2
3
4
5
6
7
8
9
10

WEDNESDAY 4

8 AM
9
10
11
12 PM
1
2
3
4
5
6
7
8
9
10

December 2013

THURSDAY 5

8 AM

9

10

11

12 PM

1

2

3

4

5

6

7

8

9

10

FRIDAY 6

8 AM

9

10

11

12 PM

1

2

3

4

5

6

7

8

9

10

SATURDAY 7

8 AM

9

10

11

12 PM

1

2

3

4

5

6

7

8

9

SUNDAY 8

8 AM

9

10

11

12 PM

1

2

3

4

5

6

7

8

9

December 2013

MONDAY 9

8 AM

9

10

11

12 PM

1

2

3

4

5

6

7

8

9

10

TUESDAY 10

8 AM

9

10

11

12 PM

1

2

3

4

5

6

7

8

9

10

WEDNESDAY 11

8 AM

9

10

11

12 PM

1

2

3

4

5

6

7

8

9

10

December 2013

THURSDAY 12

8 AM

9

10

11

12 PM

1

2

3

4

5

6

7

8

9

10

FRIDAY 13

8 AM

9

10

11

12 PM

1

2

3

4

5

6

7

8

9

10

SATURDAY 14

8 AM
9
10
11
12 PM
1
2
3
4
5
6
7
8
9

SUNDAY 15

8 AM
9
10
11
12 PM
1
2
3
4
5
6
7
8
9

December 2013

MONDAY 16	TUESDAY 17	WEDNESDAY 18
8 AM	8 AM	8 AM
9	9	9
10	10	10
11	11	11
12 PM	12 PM	12 PM
1	1	1
2	2	2
3	3	3
4	4	4
5	5	5
6	6	6
7	7	7
8	8	8
9	9	9
10	10	10

December 2013

THURSDAY 19

8 AM

9

10

11

12 PM

1

2

3

4

5

6

7

8

9

10

FRIDAY 20

8 AM

9

10

11

12 PM

1

2

3

4

5

6

7

8

9

10

SATURDAY 21

8 AM

9

10

11

12 PM

1

2

3

4

5

6

7

8

9

SUNDAY 22

8 AM

9

10

11

12 PM

1

2

3

4

5

6

7

8

9

December 2013

MONDAY 23	TUESDAY 24	WEDNESDAY 25
	Christmas Eve	Christmas Day [f]
8 AM	8 AM	8 AM
9	9	9
10	10	10
11	11	11
12 PM	12 PM	12 PM
1	1	1
2	2	2
3	3	3
4	4	4
5	5	5
6	6	6
7	7	7
8	8	8
9	9	9
10	10	10

THURSDAY 26

8 AM

9

10

11

12 PM

1

2

3

4

5

6

7

8

9

10

FRIDAY 27

8 AM

9

10

11

12 PM

1

2

3

4

5

6

7

8

9

10

SATURDAY 28

8 AM
9
10
11
12 PM
1
2
3
4
5
6
7
8
9

SUNDAY 29

8 AM
9
10
11
12 PM
1
2
3
4
5
6
7
8
9

December 2013

MONDAY 30	TUESDAY 31	WEDNESDAY 1
		New Year's Day [f]
8 AM	8 AM	8 AM
9	9	9
10	10	10
11	11	11
12 PM	12 PM	12 PM
1	1	1
2	2	2
3	3	3
4	4	4
5	5	5
6	6	6
7	7	7
8	8	8
9	9	9
10	10	10

January 2014

THURSDAY 2

8 AM
9
10
11
12 PM
1
2
3
4
5
6
7
8
9
10

FRIDAY 3

8 AM
9
10
11
12 PM
1
2
3
4
5
6
7
8
9
10

SATURDAY 4

8 AM
9
10
11
12 PM
1
2
3
4
5
6
7
8
9

SUNDAY 5

8 AM
9
10
11
12 PM
1
2
3
4
5
6
7
8
9

January 2014

MONDAY 6

8 AM

9

10

11

12 PM

1

2

3

4

5

6

7

8

9

10

TUESDAY 7

8 AM

9

10

11

12 PM

1

2

3

4

5

6

7

8

9

10

WEDNESDAY 8

8 AM

9

10

11

12 PM

1

2

3

4

5

6

7

8

9

10

January 2014

THURSDAY 9	FRIDAY 10
8 AM	8 AM
9	9
10	10
11	11
12 PM	12 PM
1	1
2	2
3	3
4	4
5	5
6	6
7	7
8	8
9	9
10	10

SATURDAY 11

8 AM
9
10
11
12 PM
1
2
3
4
5
6
7
8
9

SUNDAY 12

8 AM
9
10
11
12 PM
1
2
3
4
5
6
7
8
9

January 2014

MONDAY 13	TUESDAY 14	WEDNESDAY 15
8 AM	8 AM	8 AM
9	9	9
10	10	10
11	11	11
12 PM	12 PM	12 PM
1	1	1
2	2	2
3	3	3
4	4	4
5	5	5
6	6	6
7	7	7
8	8	8
9	9	9
10	10	10

THURSDAY 16

8 AM
9
10
11
12 PM
1
2
3
4
5
6
7
8
9
10

FRIDAY 17

8 AM
9
10
11
12 PM
1
2
3
4
5
6
7
8
9
10

SATURDAY 18

8 AM
9
10
11
12 PM
1
2
3
4
5
6
7
8
9

SUNDAY 19

8 AM
9
10
11
12 PM
1
2
3
4
5
6
7
8
9

January 2014

MONDAY 20

8 AM
9
10
11
12 PM
1
2
3
4
5
6
7
8
9
10

TUESDAY 21

8 AM
9
10
11
12 PM
1
2
3
4
5
6
7
8
9
10

WEDNESDAY 22

8 AM
9
10
11
12 PM
1
2
3
4
5
6
7
8
9
10

THURSDAY 23

8 AM
9
10
11
12 PM
1
2
3
4
5
6
7
8
9
10

FRIDAY 24

8 AM
9
10
11
12 PM
1
2
3
4
5
6
7
8
9
10

SATURDAY 25

8 AM
9
10
11
12 PM
1
2
3
4
5
6
7
8
9

SUNDAY 26

8 AM
9
10
11
12 PM
1
2
3
4
5
6
7
8
9

January 2014

MONDAY 27	TUESDAY 28	WEDNESDAY 29
8 AM	8 AM	8 AM
9	9	9
10	10	10
11	11	11
12 PM	12 PM	12 PM
1	1	1
2	2	2
3	3	3
4	4	4
5	5	5
6	6	6
7	7	7
8	8	8
9	9	9
10	10	10

February 2014

THURSDAY 30

8 AM
9
10
11
12 PM
1
2
3
4
5
6
7
8
9
10

FRIDAY 31

8 AM
9
10
11
12 PM
1
2
3
4
5
6
7
8
9
10

SATURDAY 1

8 AM
9
10
11
12 PM
1
2
3
4
5
6
7
8
9

SUNDAY 2

8 AM
9
10
11
12 PM
1
2
3
4
5
6
7
8
9

February 2014

MONDAY 3

8 AM
9
10
11
12 PM
1
2
3
4
5
6
7
8
9
10

TUESDAY 4

8 AM
9
10
11
12 PM
1
2
3
4
5
6
7
8
9
10

WEDNESDAY 5

8 AM
9
10
11
12 PM
1
2
3
4
5
6
7
8
9
10

THURSDAY 6

8 AM
9
10
11
12 PM
1
2
3
4
5
6
7
8
9
10

FRIDAY 7

8 AM
9
10
11
12 PM
1
2
3
4
5
6
7
8
9
10

SATURDAY 8

8 AM
9
10
11
12 PM
1
2
3
4
5
6
7
8
9

SUNDAY 9

8 AM
9
10
11
12 PM
1
2
3
4
5
6
7
8
9

February 2014

MONDAY 10	TUESDAY 11	WEDNESDAY 12
8 AM	8 AM	8 AM
9	9	9
10	10	10
11	11	11
12 PM	12 PM	12 PM
1	1	1
2	2	2
3	3	3
4	4	4
5	5	5
6	6	6
7	7	7
8	8	8
9	9	9
10	10	10

THURSDAY 13

8 AM

9

10

11

12 PM

1

2

3

4

5

6

7

8

9

10

FRIDAY 14

Valentine's Day

8 AM

9

10

11

12 PM

1

2

3

4

5

6

7

8

9

10

SATURDAY 15

8 AM

9

10

11

12 PM

1

2

3

4

5

6

7

8

9

SUNDAY 16

8 AM

9

10

11

12 PM

1

2

3

4

5

6

7

8

9

February 2014

MONDAY 17

President's Day [f]

8 AM

9

10

11

12 PM

1

2

3

4

5

6

7

8

9

10

TUESDAY 18

8 AM

9

10

11

12 PM

1

2

3

4

5

6

7

8

9

10

WEDNESDAY 19

8 AM

9

10

11

12 PM

1

2

3

4

5

6

7

8

9

10

February 2014

THURSDAY 20

8 AM

9

10

11

12 PM

1

2

3

4

5

6

7

8

9

10

FRIDAY 21

8 AM

9

10

11

12 PM

1

2

3

4

5

6

7

8

9

10

SATURDAY 22

8 AM

9

10

11

12 PM

1

2

3

4

5

6

7

8

9

SUNDAY 23

8 AM

9

10

11

12 PM

1

2

3

4

5

6

7

8

9

February 2014

MONDAY 24

8 AM
9
10
11
12 PM
1
2
3
4
5
6
7
8
9
10

TUESDAY 25

8 AM
9
10
11
12 PM
1
2
3
4
5
6
7
8
9
10

WEDNESDAY 26

8 AM
9
10
11
12 PM
1
2
3
4
5
6
7
8
9
10

March 2014

THURSDAY 27

8 AM
9
10
11
12 PM
1
2
3
4
5
6
7
8
9
10

FRIDAY 28

8 AM
9
10
11
12 PM
1
2
3
4
5
6
7
8
9
10

SATURDAY 1

8 AM
9
10
11
12 PM
1
2
3
4
5
6
7
8
9

SUNDAY 2

8 AM
9
10
11
12 PM
1
2
3
4
5
6
7
8
9

March 2014

MONDAY 3	TUESDAY 4	WEDNESDAY 5
8 AM	8 AM	8 AM
9	9	9
10	10	10
11	11	11
12 PM	12 PM	12 PM
1	1	1
2	2	2
3	3	3
4	4	4
5	5	5
6	6	6
7	7	7
8	8	8
9	9	9
10	10	10

March 2014

THURSDAY 6

8 AM

9

10

11

12 PM

1

2

3

4

5

6

7

8

9

10

FRIDAY 7

8 AM

9

10

11

12 PM

1

2

3

4

5

6

7

8

9

10

SATURDAY 8

8 AM

9

10

11

12 PM

1

2

3

4

5

6

7

8

9

SUNDAY 9

Daylight Savings Time (+ 1hr.)

8 AM

9

10

11

12 PM

1

2

3

4

5

6

7

8

9

March 2014

MONDAY 10	TUESDAY 11	WEDNESDAY 12
8 AM	8 AM	8 AM
9	9	9
10	10	10
11	11	11
12 PM	12 PM	12 PM
1	1	1
2	2	2
3	3	3
4	4	4
5	5	5
6	6	6
7	7	7
8	8	8
9	9	9
10	10	10

THURSDAY 13

8 AM

9

10

11

12 PM

1

2

3

4

5

6

7

8

9

10

FRIDAY 14

8 AM

9

10

11

12 PM

1

2

3

4

5

6

7

8

9

10

SATURDAY 15

8 AM
9
10
11
12 PM
1
2
3
4
5
6
7
8
9

SUNDAY 16

8 AM
9
10
11
12 PM
1
2
3
4
5
6
7
8
9

March 2014

MONDAY 17

St. Patrick's Day

8 AM

9

10

11

12 PM

1

2

3

4

5

6

7

8

9

10

TUESDAY 18

8 AM

9

10

11

12 PM

1

2

3

4

5

6

7

8

9

10

WEDNESDAY 19

8 AM

9

10

11

12 PM

1

2

3

4

5

6

7

8

9

10

March 2014

THURSDAY 20

Vernal Equinox

8 AM

9

10

11

12 PM

1

2

3

4

5

6

7

8

9

10

FRIDAY 21

8 AM

9

10

11

12 PM

1

2

3

4

5

6

7

8

9

10

SATURDAY 22

8 AM

9

10

11

12 PM

1

2

3

4

5

6

7

8

9

SUNDAY 23

8 AM

9

10

11

12 PM

1

2

3

4

5

6

7

8

9

March 2014

MONDAY 24

8 AM
9
10
11
12 PM
1
2
3
4
5
6
7
8
9
10

TUESDAY 25

8 AM
9
10
11
12 PM
1
2
3
4
5
6
7
8
9
10

WEDNESDAY 26

8 AM
9
10
11
12 PM
1
2
3
4
5
6
7
8
9
10

March 2014

THURSDAY 27

8 AM

9

10

11

12 PM

1

2

3

4

5

6

7

8

9

10

FRIDAY 28

8 AM

9

10

11

12 PM

1

2

3

4

5

6

7

8

9

10

SATURDAY 29

8 AM

9

10

11

12 PM

1

2

3

4

5

6

7

8

9

SUNDAY 30

8 AM

9

10

11

12 PM

1

2

3

4

5

6

7

8

9

March 2014

MONDAY 31

8 AM
9
10
11
12 PM
1
2
3
4
5
6
7
8
9
10

TUESDAY 1

8 AM
9
10
11
12 PM
1
2
3
4
5
6
7
8
9
10

WEDNESDAY 2

8 AM
9
10
11
12 PM
1
2
3
4
5
6
7
8
9
10

April 2014

THURSDAY 3

8 AM

9

10

11

12 PM

1

2

3

4

5

6

7

8

9

10

FRIDAY 4

8 AM

9

10

11

12 PM

1

2

3

4

5

6

7

8

9

10

SATURDAY 5

8 AM

9

10

11

12 PM

1

2

3

4

5

6

7

8

9

SUNDAY 6

8 AM

9

10

11

12 PM

1

2

3

4

5

6

7

8

9

April 2014

MONDAY 7	TUESDAY 8	WEDNESDAY 9
8 AM	8 AM	8 AM
9	9	9
10	10	10
11	11	11
12 PM	12 PM	12 PM
1	1	1
2	2	2
3	3	3
4	4	4
5	5	5
6	6	6
7	7	7
8	8	8
9	9	9
10	10	10

April 2014

THURSDAY 10

8 AM
9
10
11
12 PM
1
2
3
4
5
6
7
8
9
10

FRIDAY 11

8 AM
9
10
11
12 PM
1
2
3
4
5
6
7
8
9
10

SATURDAY 12

8 AM
9
10
11
12 PM
1
2
3
4
5
6
7
8
9

SUNDAY 13
Palm Sunday

8 AM
9
10
11
12 PM
1
2
3
4
5
6
7
8
9

April 2014

MONDAY 14

Passover (begins at sundown)

8 AM

9

10

11

12 PM

1

2

3

4

5

6

7

8

9

10

TUESDAY 15

8 AM

9

10

11

12 PM

1

2

3

4

5

6

7

8

9

10

WEDNESDAY 16

8 AM

9

10

11

12 PM

1

2

3

4

5

6

7

8

9

10

April 2014

THURSDAY 17

8 AM

9

10

11

12 PM

1

2

3

4

5

6

7

8

9

10

FRIDAY 18

Good Friday

8 AM

9

10

11

12 PM

1

2

3

4

5

6

7

8

9

10

SATURDAY 19

Holy Saturday

8 AM

9

10

11

12 PM

1

2

3

4

5

6

7

8

9

SUNDAY 20

Easter Sunday

8 AM

9

10

11

12 PM

1

2

3

4

5

6

7

8

9

April 2014

MONDAY 21

8 AM

9

10

11

12 PM

1

2

3

4

5

6

7

8

9

10

TUESDAY 22

Passover (ends at nightfall)

8 AM

9

10

11

12 PM

1

2

3

4

5

6

7

8

9

10

WEDNESDAY 23

8 AM

9

10

11

12 PM

1

2

3

4

5

6

7

8

9

10

April 2014

THURSDAY 24

8 AM

9

10

11

12 PM

1

2

3

4

5

6

7

8

9

10

FRIDAY 25

Arbor Day

8 AM

9

10

11

12 PM

1

2

3

4

5

6

7

8

9

10

SATURDAY 26

8 AM
9
10
11
12 PM
1
2
3
4
5
6
7
8
9

SUNDAY 27

8 AM
9
10
11
12 PM
1
2
3
4
5
6
7
8
9

April 2014

MONDAY 28

Yom HaShoah (Holocaust Memorial Day)

8 AM

9

10

11

12 PM

1

2

3

4

5

6

7

8

9

10

TUESDAY 29

8 AM

9

10

11

12 PM

1

2

3

4

5

6

7

8

9

10

WEDNESDAY 30

8 AM

9

10

11

12 PM

1

2

3

4

5

6

7

8

9

10

May 2014

THURSDAY 1

8 AM
9
10
11
12 PM
1
2
3
4
5
6
7
8
9
10

FRIDAY 2

8 AM
9
10
11
12 PM
1
2
3
4
5
6
7
8
9
10

SATURDAY 3

8 AM
9
10
11
12 PM
1
2
3
4
5
6
7
8
9

SUNDAY 4

8 AM
9
10
11
12 PM
1
2
3
4
5
6
7
8
9

May 2014

MONDAY 5	TUESDAY 6	WEDNESDAY 7
8 AM	8 AM	8 AM
9	9	9
10	10	10
11	11	11
12 PM	12 PM	12 PM
1	1	1
2	2	2
3	3	3
4	4	4
5	5	5
6	6	6
7	7	7
8	8	8
9	9	9
10	10	10

May 2014

THURSDAY 8

8 AM
9
10
11
12 PM
1
2
3
4
5
6
7
8
9
10

FRIDAY 9

8 AM
9
10
11
12 PM
1
2
3
4
5
6
7
8
9
10

SATURDAY 10

8 AM
9
10
11
12 PM
1
2
3
4
5
6
7
8
9

SUNDAY 11

Mother's Day

8 AM
9
10
11
12 PM
1
2
3
4
5
6
7
8
9

May 2014

MONDAY 12

8 AM

9

10

11

12 PM

1

2

3

4

5

6

7

8

9

10

TUESDAY 13

8 AM

9

10

11

12 PM

1

2

3

4

5

6

7

8

9

10

WEDNESDAY 14

Second Passover

8 AM

9

10

11

12 PM

1

2

3

4

5

6

7

8

9

10

May 2014

THURSDAY 15

8 AM

9

10

11

12 PM

1

2

3

4

5

6

7

8

9

10

FRIDAY 16

8 AM

9

10

11

12 PM

1

2

3

4

5

6

7

8

9

10

SATURDAY 17

Armed Forces Day

8 AM

9

10

11

12 PM

1

2

3

4

5

6

7

8

9

SUNDAY 18

8 AM

9

10

11

12 PM

1

2

3

4

5

6

7

8

9

May 2014

MONDAY 19	TUESDAY 20	WEDNESDAY 21
8 AM	8 AM	8 AM
9	9	9
10	10	10
11	11	11
12 PM	12 PM	12 PM
1	1	1
2	2	2
3	3	3
4	4	4
5	5	5
6	6	6
7	7	7
8	8	8
9	9	9
10	10	10

THURSDAY 22

8 AM
9
10
11
12 PM
1
2
3
4
5
6
7
8
9
10

FRIDAY 23

8 AM
9
10
11
12 PM
1
2
3
4
5
6
7
8
9
10

SATURDAY 24

8 AM
9
10
11
12 PM
1
2
3
4
5
6
7
8
9

SUNDAY 25

8 AM
9
10
11
12 PM
1
2
3
4
5
6
7
8
9

May 2014

MONDAY 26

Memorial Day [f]

8 AM

9

10

11

12 PM

1

2

3

4

5

6

7

8

9

10

** Memorial Day originated in the 19th century as a day to remember the soldiers who gave their lives in the American Civil War.*

TUESDAY 27

8 AM

9

10

11

12 PM

1

2

3

4

5

6

7

8

9

10

WEDNESDAY 28

8 AM

9

10

11

12 PM

1

2

3

4

5

6

7

8

9

10

THURSDAY 29

8 AM

9

10

11

12 PM

1

2

3

4

5

6

7

8

9

10

FRIDAY 30

8 AM

9

10

11

12 PM

1

2

3

4

5

6

7

8

9

10

SATURDAY 31

8 AM
9
10
11
12 PM
1
2
3
4
5
6
7
8
9

SUNDAY 1

8 AM
9
10
11
12 PM
1
2
3
4
5
6
7
8
9

June 2014

MONDAY 2

8 AM

9

10

11

12 PM

1

2

3

4

5

6

7

8

9

10

TUESDAY 3

Shavout (begins at sunset)

8 AM

9

10

11

12 PM

1

2

3

4

5

6

7

8

9

10

WEDNESDAY 4

8 AM

9

10

11

12 PM

1

2

3

4

5

6

7

8

9

10

THURSDAY 5

Shavout (ends at nightfall)

8 AM
9
10
11
12 PM
1
2
3
4
5
6
7
8
9
10

FRIDAY 6

D-Day (June 6, 1944)

8 AM
9
10
11
12 PM
1
2
3
4
5
6
7
8
9
10

SATURDAY 7

8 AM
9
10
11
12 PM
1
2
3
4
5
6
7
8
9

SUNDAY 8

8 AM
9
10
11
12 PM
1
2
3
4
5
6
7
8
9

June 2014

MONDAY 9

8 AM

9

10

11

12 PM

1

2

3

4

5

6

7

8

9

10

TUESDAY 10

8 AM

9

10

11

12 PM

1

2

3

4

5

6

7

8

9

10

WEDNESDAY 11

Kamehameha Day (Hawaii)

8 AM

9

10

11

12 PM

1

2

3

4

5

6

7

8

9

10

June 2014

THURSDAY 12

8 AM

9

10

11

12 PM

1

2

3

4

5

6

7

8

9

10

FRIDAY 13

8 AM

9

10

11

12 PM

1

2

3

4

5

6

7

8

9

10

SATURDAY 14

8 AM

9

10

11

12 PM

1

2

3

4

5

6

7

8

9

SUNDAY 15

Father's Day

8 AM

9

10

11

12 PM

1

2

3

4

5

6

7

8

9

June 2014

MONDAY 16	TUESDAY 17	WEDNESDAY 18
8 AM	8 AM	8 AM
9	9	9
10	10	10
11	11	11
12 PM	12 PM	12 PM
1	1	1
2	2	2
3	3	3
4	4	4
5	5	5
6	6	6
7	7	7
8	8	8
9	9	9
10	10	10

June 2014

THURSDAY 19

Juneteenth Day

8 AM

9

10

11

12 PM

1

2

3

4

5

6

7

8

9

10

FRIDAY 20

8 AM

9

10

11

12 PM

1

2

3

4

5

6

7

8

9

10

SATURDAY 21

June Soltice

8 AM

9

10

11

12 PM

1

2

3

4

5

6

7

8

9

SUNDAY 22

8 AM

9

10

11

12 PM

1

2

3

4

5

6

7

8

9

June 2014

MONDAY 23	TUESDAY 24	WEDNESDAY 25
8 AM	8 AM	8 AM
9	9	9
10	10	10
11	11	11
12 PM	12 PM	12 PM
1	1	1
2	2	2
3	3	3
4	4	4
5	5	5
6	6	6
7	7	7
8	8	8
9	9	9
10	10	10

June 2014

THURSDAY 26

8 AM

9

10

11

12 PM

1

2

3

4

5

6

7

8

9

10

FRIDAY 27

8 AM

9

10

11

12 PM

1

2

3

4

5

6

7

8

9

10

SATURDAY 28

8 AM

9

10

11

12 PM

1

2

3

4

5

6

7

8

9

SUNDAY 29

Ramadan (starts)

8 AM

9

10

11

12 PM

1

2

3

4

5

6

7

8

9

June 2014

MONDAY 30	TUESDAY 1	WEDNESDAY 2
8 AM	8 AM	8 AM
9	9	9
10	10	10
11	11	11
12 PM	12 PM	12 PM
1	1	1
2	2	2
3	3	3
4	4	4
5	5	5
6	6	6
7	7	7
8	8	8
9	9	9
10	10	10

THURSDAY 3

8 AM

9

10

11

12 PM

1

2

3

4

5

6

7

8

9

10

FRIDAY 4

Independence Day [f]

8 AM

9

10

11

12 PM

1

2

3

4

5

6

7

8

9

10

** Independence Day is a federal holiday to celebrate and acknowledge the signing of the Declaration of Independence.*

SATURDAY 5

8 AM

9

10

11

12 PM

1

2

3

4

5

6

7

8

9

SUNDAY 6

8 AM

9

10

11

12 PM

1

2

3

4

5

6

7

8

9

July 2014

MONDAY 7	TUESDAY 8	WEDNESDAY 9
8 AM	8 AM	8 AM
9	9	9
10	10	10
11	11	11
12 PM	12 PM	12 PM
1	1	1
2	2	2
3	3	3
4	4	4
5	5	5
6	6	6
7	7	7
8	8	8
9	9	9
10	10	10

THURSDAY 10

8 AM

9

10

11

12 PM

1

2

3

4

5

6

7

8

9

10

FRIDAY 11

8 AM

9

10

11

12 PM

1

2

3

4

5

6

7

8

9

10

SATURDAY 12

8 AM

9

10

11

12 PM

1

2

3

4

5

6

7

8

9

SUNDAY 13

8 AM

9

10

11

12 PM

1

2

3

4

5

6

7

8

9

July 2014

MONDAY 14	TUESDAY 15	WEDNESDAY 16
8 AM	8 AM	8 AM
9	9	9
10	10	10
11	11	11
12 PM	12 PM	12 PM
1	1	1
2	2	2
3	3	3
4	4	4
5	5	5
6	6	6
7	7	7
8	8	8
9	9	9
10	10	10

July 2014

THURSDAY 17

8 AM

9

10

11

12 PM

1

2

3

4

5

6

7

8

9

10

FRIDAY 18

8 AM

9

10

11

12 PM

1

2

3

4

5

6

7

8

9

10

SATURDAY 19

8 AM

9

10

11

12 PM

1

2

3

4

5

6

7

8

9

SUNDAY 20

8 AM

9

10

11

12 PM

1

2

3

4

5

6

7

8

9

July 2014

MONDAY 21	TUESDAY 22	WEDNESDAY 23
8 AM	8 AM	8 AM
9	9	9
10	10	10
11	11	11
12 PM	12 PM	12 PM
1	1	1
2	2	2
3	3	3
4	4	4
5	5	5
6	6	6
7	7	7
8	8	8
9	9	9
10	10	10

July 2014

THURSDAY 24

8 AM

9

10

11

12 PM

1

2

3

4

5

6

7

8

9

10

FRIDAY 25

8 AM

9

10

11

12 PM

1

2

3

4

5

6

7

8

9

10

SATURDAY 26

8 AM
9
10
11
12 PM
1
2
3
4
5
6
7
8
9

SUNDAY 27

8 AM
9
10
11
12 PM
1
2
3
4
5
6
7
8
9

July 2014

MONDAY 28	TUESDAY 29	WEDNESDAY 30
8 AM	8 AM	8 AM
9	9	9
10	10	10
11	11	11
12 PM	12 PM	12 PM
1	1	1
2	2	2
3	3	3
4	4	4
5	5	5
6	6	6
7	7	7
8	8	8
9	9	9
10	10	10

August 2014

THURSDAY 31

8 AM

9

10

11

12 PM

1

2

3

4

5

6

7

8

9

10

FRIDAY 1

8 AM

9

10

11

12 PM

1

2

3

4

5

6

7

8

9

10

SATURDAY 2

8 AM

9

10

11

12 PM

1

2

3

4

5

6

7

8

9

SUNDAY 3

8 AM

9

10

11

12 PM

1

2

3

4

5

6

7

8

9

August 2014

MONDAY 4

8 AM

9

10

11

12 PM

1

2

3

4

5

6

7

8

9

10

TUESDAY 5

8 AM

9

10

11

12 PM

1

2

3

4

5

6

7

8

9

10

WEDNESDAY 6

8 AM

9

10

11

12 PM

1

2

3

4

5

6

7

8

9

10

August 2014

THURSDAY 7

8 AM

9

10

11

12 PM

1

2

3

4

5

6

7

8

9

10

FRIDAY 8

8 AM

9

10

11

12 PM

1

2

3

4

5

6

7

8

9

10

SATURDAY 9

8 AM
9
10
11
12 PM
1
2
3
4
5
6
7
8
9

SUNDAY 10

8 AM
9
10
11
12 PM
1
2
3
4
5
6
7
8
9

August 2014

MONDAY 11	TUESDAY 12	WEDNESDAY 13
Victory Day (August 9, 1945) & The 15th of Av		
8 AM	8 AM	8 AM
9	9	9
10	10	10
11	11	11
12 PM	12 PM	12 PM
1	1	1
2	2	2
3	3	3
4	4	4
5	5	5
6	6	6
7	7	7
8	8	8
9	9	9
10	10	10

August 2014

THURSDAY 14

8 AM

9

10

11

12 PM

1

2

3

4

5

6

7

8

9

10

FRIDAY 15

8 AM

9

10

11

12 PM

1

2

3

4

5

6

7

8

9

10

SATURDAY 16

8 AM

9

10

11

12 PM

1

2

3

4

5

6

7

8

9

SUNDAY 17

8 AM

9

10

11

12 PM

1

2

3

4

5

6

7

8

9

August 2014

MONDAY 18	TUESDAY 19	WEDNESDAY 20
8 AM	8 AM	8 AM
9	9	9
10	10	10
11	11	11
12 PM	12 PM	12 PM
1	1	1
2	2	2
3	3	3
4	4	4
5	5	5
6	6	6
7	7	7
8	8	8
9	9	9
10	10	10

August 2014

THURSDAY 21

8 AM

9

10

11

12 PM

1

2

3

4

5

6

7

8

9

10

FRIDAY 22

8 AM

9

10

11

12 PM

1

2

3

4

5

6

7

8

9

10

SATURDAY 23

8 AM

9

10

11

12 PM

1

2

3

4

5

6

7

8

9

SUNDAY 24

8 AM

9

10

11

12 PM

1

2

3

4

5

6

7

8

9

August 2014

MONDAY 25	TUESDAY 26	WEDNESDAY 27
8 AM	8 AM	8 AM
9	9	9
10	10	10
11	11	11
12 PM	12 PM	12 PM
1	1	1
2	2	2
3	3	3
4	4	4
5	5	5
6	6	6
7	7	7
8	8	8
9	9	9
10	10	10

August 2014

THURSDAY 28

8 AM

9

10

11

12 PM

1

2

3

4

5

6

7

8

9

10

FRIDAY 29

8 AM

9

10

11

12 PM

1

2

3

4

5

6

7

8

9

10

SATURDAY 30

8 AM

9

10

11

12 PM

1

2

3

4

5

6

7

8

9

SUNDAY 31

8 AM

9

10

11

12 PM

1

2

3

4

5

6

7

8

9

September 2014

MONDAY 1

Labor Day [f]

8 AM

9

10

11

12 PM

1

2

3

4

5

6

7

8

9

10

** Labor Day is a federal holiday meant to celebrate and acknowledge the achievements of workers and the labor movement.*

TUESDAY 2

8 AM

9

10

11

12 PM

1

2

3

4

5

6

7

8

9

10

WEDNESDAY 3

8 AM

9

10

11

12 PM

1

2

3

4

5

6

7

8

9

10

September 2014

THURSDAY 4

8 AM

9

10

11

12 PM

1

2

3

4

5

6

7

8

9

10

FRIDAY 5

8 AM

9

10

11

12 PM

1

2

3

4

5

6

7

8

9

10

SATURDAY 6

8 AM

9

10

11

12 PM

1

2

3

4

5

6

7

8

9

SUNDAY 7

8 AM

9

10

11

12 PM

1

2

3

4

5

6

7

8

9

September 2014

MONDAY 8

8 AM

9

10

11

12 PM

1

2

3

4

5

6

7

8

9

10

TUESDAY 9

8 AM

9

10

11

12 PM

1

2

3

4

5

6

7

8

9

10

WEDNESDAY 10

8 AM

9

10

11

12 PM

1

2

3

4

5

6

7

8

9

10

September 2014

THURSDAY 11

8 AM

9

10

11

12 PM

1

2

3

4

5

6

7

8

9

10

FRIDAY 12

8 AM

9

10

11

12 PM

1

2

3

4

5

6

7

8

9

10

SATURDAY 13

8 AM

9

10

11

12 PM

1

2

3

4

5

6

7

8

9

SUNDAY 14

8 AM

9

10

11

12 PM

1

2

3

4

5

6

7

8

9

September 2014

MONDAY 15

8 AM
9
10
11
12 PM
1
2
3
4
5
6
7
8
9
10

TUESDAY 16

8 AM
9
10
11
12 PM
1
2
3
4
5
6
7
8
9
10

WEDNESDAY 17

8 AM
9
10
11
12 PM
1
2
3
4
5
6
7
8
9
10

September 2014

THURSDAY 18

8 AM

9

10

11

12 PM

1

2

3

4

5

6

7

8

9

10

FRIDAY 19

8 AM

9

10

11

12 PM

1

2

3

4

5

6

7

8

9

10

SATURDAY 20

8 AM

9

10

11

12 PM

1

2

3

4

5

6

7

8

9

SUNDAY 21

8 AM

9

10

11

12 PM

1

2

3

4

5

6

7

8

9

September 2014

MONDAY 22	TUESDAY 23	WEDNESDAY 24
	Autumnal Equinox	Rosh Hashanah (begins @ sundown)
8 AM	8 AM	8 AM
9	9	9
10	10	10
11	11	11
12 PM	12 PM	12 PM
1	1	1
2	2	2
3	3	3
4	4	4
5	5	5
6	6	6
7	7	7
8	8	8
9	9	9
10	10	10
		** Rosh Hashanah is the Jewish New Year; begins the ten days of penitence culminating in Yom Kippur.*

September 2014

THURSDAY 25

8 AM

9

10

11

12 PM

1

2

3

4

5

6

7

8

9

10

FRIDAY 26

Rosh Hashanah (ends at nightfall)

8 AM

9

10

11

12 PM

1

2

3

4

5

6

7

8

9

10

SATURDAY 27

8 AM

9

10

11

12 PM

1

2

3

4

5

6

7

8

9

SUNDAY 28

8 AM

9

10

11

12 PM

1

2

3

4

5

6

7

8

9

September 2014

MONDAY 29

8 AM
9
10
11
12 PM
1
2
3
4
5
6
7
8
9
10

TUESDAY 30

8 AM
9
10
11
12 PM
1
2
3
4
5
6
7
8
9
10

WEDNESDAY 1

8 AM
9
10
11
12 PM
1
2
3
4
5
6
7
8
9
10

October 2014

THURSDAY 2

8 AM

9

10

11

12 PM

1

2

3

4

5

6

7

8

9

10

FRIDAY 3

Yom Kippur (begins at sundown)

8 AM

9

10

11

12 PM

1

2

3

4

5

6

7

8

9

10

**Yom Kippur (Day of Atonement) is the most solemn fast of the Jewish year; the last of the ten days of penitence that begin with Rosh Hashanah (the Jewish New Year).*

SATURDAY 4

Yom Kippur (ends at nightfall)

8 AM

9

10

11

12 PM

1

2

3

4

5

6

7

8

9

SUNDAY 5

8 AM

9

10

11

12 PM

1

2

3

4

5

6

7

8

9

October 2014

MONDAY 6	TUESDAY 7	WEDNESDAY 8
		Sukkot (begins at sunset)
8 AM	8 AM	8 AM
9	9	9
10	10	10
11	11	11
12 PM	12 PM	12 PM
1	1	1
2	2	2
3	3	3
4	4	4
5	5	5
6	6	6
7	7	7
8	8	8
9	9	9
10	10	10

October 2014

THURSDAY 9

8 AM

9

10

11

12 PM

1

2

3

4

5

6

7

8

9

10

FRIDAY 10

8 AM

9

10

11

12 PM

1

2

3

4

5

6

7

8

9

10

SATURDAY 11

8 AM

9

10

11

12 PM

1

2

3

4

5

6

7

8

9

SUNDAY 12

8 AM

9

10

11

12 PM

1

2

3

4

5

6

7

8

9

October 2014

MONDAY 13	TUESDAY 14	WEDNESDAY 15
Columbus Day & Native American's Day [f]		Sukkot (ends at nightfall)
8 AM	8 AM	8 AM
9	9	9
10	10	10
11	11	11
12 PM	12 PM	12 PM
1	1	1
2	2	2
3	3	3
4	4	4
5	5	5
6	6	6
7	7	7
8	8	8
9	9	9
10	10	10

October 2014

THURSDAY 16

Boss's Day (take a holiday)

8 AM

9

10

11

12 PM

1

2

3

4

5

6

7

8

9

10

FRIDAY 17

8 AM

9

10

11

12 PM

1

2

3

4

5

6

7

8

9

10

SATURDAY 18

8 AM

9

10

11

12 PM

1

2

3

4

5

6

7

8

9

SUNDAY 19

8 AM

9

10

11

12 PM

1

2

3

4

5

6

7

8

9

October 2014

MONDAY 20

8 AM
9
10
11
12 PM
1
2
3
4
5
6
7
8
9
10

TUESDAY 21

8 AM
9
10
11
12 PM
1
2
3
4
5
6
7
8
9
10

WEDNESDAY 22

8 AM
9
10
11
12 PM
1
2
3
4
5
6
7
8
9
10

October 2014

THURSDAY 23

8 AM

9

10

11

12 PM

1

2

3

4

5

6

7

8

9

10

FRIDAY 24

8 AM

9

10

11

12 PM

1

2

3

4

5

6

7

8

9

10

SATURDAY 25

8 AM

9

10

11

12 PM

1

2

3

4

5

6

7

8

9

SUNDAY 26

8 AM

9

10

11

12 PM

1

2

3

4

5

6

7

8

9

October 2014

MONDAY 27	TUESDAY 28	WEDNESDAY 29
8 AM	8 AM	8 AM
9	9	9
10	10	10
11	11	11
12 PM	12 PM	12 PM
1	1	1
2	2	2
3	3	3
4	4	4
5	5	5
6	6	6
7	7	7
8	8	8
9	9	9
10	10	10

November 2014

THURSDAY 30

8 AM

9

10

11

12 PM

1

2

3

4

5

6

7

8

9

10

FRIDAY 31

Halloween

8 AM

9

10

11

12 PM

1

2

3

4

5

6

7

8

9

10

SATURDAY 1

All Saints Day

8 AM

9

10

11

12 PM

1

2

3

4

5

6

7

8

9

SUNDAY 2

Day Light Savings Time (- 1 hr.)

8 AM

9

10

11

12 PM

1

2

3

4

5

6

7

8

9

November 2014

MONDAY 3	TUESDAY 4	WEDNESDAY 5
8 AM	8 AM	8 AM
9	9	9
10	10	10
11	11	11
12 PM	12 PM	12 PM
1	1	1
2	2	2
3	3	3
4	4	4
5	5	5
6	6	6
7	7	7
8	8	8
9	9	9
10	10	10

THURSDAY 6

8 AM

9

10

11

12 PM

1

2

3

4

5

6

7

8

9

10

FRIDAY 7

8 AM

9

10

11

12 PM

1

2

3

4

5

6

7

8

9

10

SATURDAY 8

8 AM

9

10

11

12 PM

1

2

3

4

5

6

7

8

9

SUNDAY 9

8 AM

9

10

11

12 PM

1

2

3

4

5

6

7

8

9

November 2014

MONDAY 10

8 AM

9

10

11

12 PM

1

2

3

4

5

6

7

8

9

10

TUESDAY 11

Veteran's Day [f]

8 AM

9

10

11

12 PM

1

2

3

4

5

6

7

8

9

10

WEDNESDAY 12

8 AM

9

10

11

12 PM

1

2

3

4

5

6

7

8

9

10

November 2014

THURSDAY 13

8 AM

9

10

11

12 PM

1

2

3

4

5

6

7

8

9

10

FRIDAY 14

8 AM

9

10

11

12 PM

1

2

3

4

5

6

7

8

9

10

SATURDAY 15

8 AM

9

10

11

12 PM

1

2

3

4

5

6

7

8

9

SUNDAY 16

8 AM

9

10

11

12 PM

1

2

3

4

5

6

7

8

9

November 2014

MONDAY 17

8 AM

9

10

11

12 PM

1

2

3

4

5

6

7

8

9

10

TUESDAY 18

8 AM

9

10

11

12 PM

1

2

3

4

5

6

7

8

9

10

WEDNESDAY 19

8 AM

9

10

11

12 PM

1

2

3

4

5

6

7

8

9

10

November 2014

THURSDAY 20

8 AM

9

10

11

12 PM

1

2

3

4

5

6

7

8

9

10

** Black Consciousness Day, Brazil*
Annual rememberance to reflect on the injustices of slavery; Brazil received 4.9 million slaves through Atlantic trade; 21.5% went to Americas.

FRIDAY 21

8 AM

9

10

11

12 PM

1

2

3

4

5

6

7

8

9

10

SATURDAY 22

8 AM

9

10

11

12 PM

1

2

3

4

5

6

7

8

9

SUNDAY 23

8 AM

9

10

11

12 PM

1

2

3

4

5

6

7

8

9

November 2014

MONDAY 24

8 AM
9
10
11
12 PM
1
2
3
4
5
6
7
8
9
10

TUESDAY 25

8 AM
9
10
11
12 PM
1
2
3
4
5
6
7
8
9
10

WEDNESDAY 26

8 AM
9
10
11
12 PM
1
2
3
4
5
6
7
8
9
10

THURSDAY 27

Thanksgiving Day [f]

8 AM

9

10

11

12 PM

1

2

3

4

5

6

7

8

9

10

FRIDAY 28

8 AM

9

10

11

12 PM

1

2

3

4

5

6

7

8

9

10

SATURDAY 29

8 AM

9

10

11

12 PM

1

2

3

4

5

6

7

8

9

SUNDAY 30

8 AM

9

10

11

12 PM

1

2

3

4

5

6

7

8

9

December 2014

MONDAY 1	TUESDAY 2	WEDNESDAY 3
8 AM	8 AM	8 AM
9	9	9
10	10	10
11	11	11
12 PM	12 PM	12 PM
1	1	1
2	2	2
3	3	3
4	4	4
5	5	5
6	6	6
7	7	7
8	8	8
9	9	9
10	10	10

December 2014

THURSDAY 4

8 AM

9

10

11

12 PM

1

2

3

4

5

6

7

8

9

10

FRIDAY 5

8 AM

9

10

11

12 PM

1

2

3

4

5

6

7

8

9

10

SATURDAY 6

8 AM

9

10

11

12 PM

1

2

3

4

5

6

7

8

9

SUNDAY 7

8 AM

9

10

11

12 PM

1

2

3

4

5

6

7

8

9

December 2014

MONDAY 8

8 AM

9

10

11

12 PM

1

2

3

4

5

6

7

8

9

10

TUESDAY 9

8 AM

9

10

11

12 PM

1

2

3

4

5

6

7

8

9

10

WEDNESDAY 10

8 AM

9

10

11

12 PM

1

2

3

4

5

6

7

8

9

10

THURSDAY 11

8 AM

9

10

11

12 PM

1

2

3

4

5

6

7

8

9

10

FRIDAY 12

8 AM

9

10

11

12 PM

1

2

3

4

5

6

7

8

9

10

SATURDAY 13

8 AM
9
10
11
12 PM
1
2
3
4
5
6
7
8
9

SUNDAY 14

8 AM
9
10
11
12 PM
1
2
3
4
5
6
7
8
9

December 2014

MONDAY 15	TUESDAY 16	WEDNESDAY 17
	Chanukah (begins at sundown)	Chanukah, 1st candle.
8 AM	8 AM	8 AM
9	9	9
10	10	10
11	11	11
12 PM	12 PM	12 PM
1	1	1
2	2	2
3	3	3
4	4	4
5	5	5
6	6	6
7	7	7
8	8	8
9	9	9
10	10	10

THURSDAY 18

Chanukah, 2nd candle.

8 AM

9

10

11

12 PM

1

2

3

4

5

6

7

8

9

10

FRIDAY 19

Chanukah, 3rd candle.

8 AM

9

10

11

12 PM

1

2

3

4

5

6

7

8

9

10

SATURDAY 20

Chanukah, 4th candle.

8 AM

9

10

11

12 PM

1

2

3

4

5

6

7

8

9

SUNDAY 21

Chanukah, 5th candle.

8 AM

9

10

11

12 PM

1

2

3

4

5

6

7

8

9

December 2014

MONDAY 22

Chanukah, 6th candle.

8 AM

9

10

11

12 PM

1

2

3

4

5

6

7

8

9

10

TUESDAY 23

Chanukah, 7th candle.

8 AM

9

10

11

12 PM

1

2

3

4

5

6

7

8

9

10

WEDNESDAY 24

Chanukah, 8th candle & Christmas Eve

8 AM

9

10

11

12 PM

1

2

3

4

5

6

7

8

9

10

THURSDAY 25

Christmas Day [f]

8 AM

9

10

11

12 PM

1

2

3

4

5

6

7

8

9

10

FRIDAY 26

Kwanzaa (until January 1)

8 AM

9

10

11

12 PM

1

2

3

4

5

6

7

8

9

10

SATURDAY 27

8 AM

9

10

11

12 PM

1

2

3

4

5

6

7

8

9

SUNDAY 28

8 AM

9

10

11

12 PM

1

2

3

4

5

6

7

8

9

December 2014

MONDAY 29

8 AM

9

10

11

12 PM

1

2

3

4

5

6

7

8

9

10

TUESDAY 30

8 AM

9

10

11

12 PM

1

2

3

4

5

6

7

8

9

10

WEDNESDAY 31

New Year's Eve

8 AM

9

10

11

12 PM

1

2

3

4

5

6

7

8

9

10

January 2015

THURSDAY 1

New Year's Day [f]

8 AM

9

10

11

12 PM

1

2

3

4

5

6

7

8

9

10

FRIDAY 2

8 AM

9

10

11

12 PM

1

2

3

4

5

6

7

8

9

10

SATURDAY 3

8 AM

9

10

11

12 PM

1

2

3

4

5

6

7

8

9

SUNDAY 4

8 AM

9

10

11

12 PM

1

2

3

4

5

6

7

8

9

January 2015

MONDAY 5	TUESDAY 6	WEDNESDAY 7
8 AM	8 AM	8 AM
9	9	9
10	10	10
11	11	11
12 PM	12 PM	12 PM
1	1	1
2	2	2
3	3	3
4	4	4
5	5	5
6	6	6
7	7	7
8	8	8
9	9	9
10	10	10

January 2015

THURSDAY 8

8 AM

9

10

11

12 PM

1

2

3

4

5

6

7

8

9

10

FRIDAY 9

8 AM

9

10

11

12 PM

1

2

3

4

5

6

7

8

9

10

SATURDAY 10

8 AM

9

10

11

12 PM

1

2

3

4

5

6

7

8

9

SUNDAY 11

8 AM

9

10

11

12 PM

1

2

3

4

5

6

7

8

9

January 2015

MONDAY 12

8 AM

9

10

11

12 PM

1

2

3

4

5

6

7

8

9

10

TUESDAY 13

8 AM

9

10

11

12 PM

1

2

3

4

5

6

7

8

9

10

WEDNESDAY 14

8 AM

9

10

11

12 PM

1

2

3

4

5

6

7

8

9

10

January 2015

THURSDAY 15

8 AM

9

10

11

12 PM

1

2

3

4

5

6

7

8

9

10

FRIDAY 16

8 AM

9

10

11

12 PM

1

2

3

4

5

6

7

8

9

10

SATURDAY 17

8 AM

9

10

11

12 PM

1

2

3

4

5

6

7

8

9

SUNDAY 18

8 AM

9

10

11

12 PM

1

2

3

4

5

6

7

8

9

January 2015

MONDAY 19

Martin Luther King Day [f]

8 AM

9

10

11

12 PM

1

2

3

4

5

6

7

8

9

10

TUESDAY 20

8 AM

9

10

11

12 PM

1

2

3

4

5

6

7

8

9

10

WEDNESDAY 21

8 AM

9

10

11

12 PM

1

2

3

4

5

6

7

8

9

10

January 2015

THURSDAY 22

8 AM

9

10

11

12 PM

1

2

3

4

5

6

7

8

9

10

FRIDAY 23

8 AM

9

10

11

12 PM

1

2

3

4

5

6

7

8

9

10

SATURDAY 24

8 AM
9
10
11
12 PM
1
2
3
4
5
6
7
8
9

SUNDAY 25

8 AM
9
10
11
12 PM
1
2
3
4
5
6
7
8
9

January 2015

MONDAY 26

8 AM

9

10

11

12 PM

1

2

3

4

5

6

7

8

9

10

TUESDAY 27

8 AM

9

10

11

12 PM

1

2

3

4

5

6

7

8

9

10

WEDNESDAY 28

8 AM

9

10

11

12 PM

1

2

3

4

5

6

7

8

9

10

February 2015

THURSDAY 29

8 AM

9

10

11

12 PM

1

2

3

4

5

6

7

8

9

10

FRIDAY 30

8 AM

9

10

11

12 PM

1

2

3

4

5

6

7

8

9

10

SATURDAY 31

8 AM

9

10

11

12 PM

1

2

3

4

5

6

7

8

9

SUNDAY 1

8 AM

9

10

11

12 PM

1

2

3

4

5

6

7

8

9

2015 PLANNER

JANUARY

1
2
3
4
5
6
7
8
9
10
11
12
13
14
15
16
17
18
19
20
21
22
23
24
25
26
27
28
29
30
31

FEBRUARY

1
2
3
4
5
6
7
8
9
10
11
12
13
14
15
16
17
18
19
20
21
22
23
24
25
26
27
28

MARCH

1
2
3
4
5
6
7
8
9
10
11
12
13
14
15
16
17
18
19
20
21
22
23
24
25
26
27
28
29
30
31

2015 PLANNER

APRIL	MAY	JUNE
1	1	1
2	2	2
3	3	3
4	4	4
5	5	5
6	6	6
7	7	7
8	8	8
9	9	9
10	10	10
11	11	11
12	12	12
13	13	13
14	14	14
15	15	15
16	16	16
17	17	17
18	18	18
19	19	19
20	20	20
21	21	21
22	22	22
23	23	23
24	24	24
25	25	25
26	26	26
27	27	27
28	28	28
29	29	29
30	30	30
	31	

2015 PLANNER

JULY

1
2
3
4
5
6
7
8
9
10
11
12
13
14
15
16
17
18
19
20
21
22
23
24
25
26
27
28
29
30
31

AUGUST

1
2
3
4
5
6
7
8
9
10
11
12
13
14
15
16
17
18
19
20
21
22
23
24
25
26
27
28
29
30
31

SEPTEMBER

1
2
3
4
5
6
7
8
9
10
11
12
13
14
15
16
17
18
19
20
21
22
23
24
25
26
27
28
29
30

2015 PLANNER

OCTOBER

1
2
3
4
5
6
7
8
9
10
11
12
13
14
15
16
17
18
19
20
21
22
23
24
25
26
27
28
29
30
31

NOVEMBER

1
2
3
4
5
6
7
8
9
10
11
12
13
14
15
16
17
18
19
20
21
22
23
24
25
26
27
28
29
30

DECEMBER

1
2
3
4
5
6
7
8
9
10
11
12
13
14
15
16
17
18
19
20
21
22
23
24
25
26
27
28
29
30
31

WEIGHTS AND MEASUREMENTS

(Key: 1 inch = 25.40 millimetres, 1 millimetre = 0.0394 inches etc.)

Inches		Millimetres	Feet		Metres	Yards		Metres	Miles		Kilometres
0.039	1	25.40	3.281	1	0.305	1.094	1	0.914	0.621	1	1.609
0.079	2	50.80	6.562	2	0.610	2.187	2	1.829	1.243	2	3.219
0.118	3	76.20	9.843	3	0.914	3.281	3	2.743	1.864	3	4.828
0.157	4	101.60	13.123	4	1.219	4.375	4	3.658	2.485	4	6.437
0.197	5	127.00	16.404	5	1.524	5.468	5	4.572	3.107	5	8.047

Sq.Feet		Sq. Metres	Sq. Yards		Sq.Metres	Cu. Feet		Cu. Metres	Cu. Yards		Cu. Metres
10.764	1	0.093	1.196	1	0.836	35.315	1	0.028	1.308	1	0.765
21.528	2	0.186	2.392	2	1.672	70.629	2	0.057	2.616	2	1.529
32.292	3	0.279	3.588	3	2.508	105.943	3	0.085	3.924	3	2.294
43.056	4	0.372	4.784	4	3.345	141.258	4	0.113	5.232	4	3.058
53.819	5	0.465	5.980	5	4.181	176.572	5	0.142	6.540	5	3.823

Pints		Litres	Gallons		Litres	Ounces		Grams	Pounds		Kilograms
1.76	1	0.568	0.220	1	4.546	0.035	1	28.350	2.205	1	0.454
3.521	2	1.136	0.440	2	9.092	0.071	2	56.699	4.409	2	0.907
5.282	3	1.704	0.660	3	13.638	0.106	3	85.049	6.614	3	1.361
7.043	4	2.272	0.880	4	18.184	0.141	4	113.398	8.819	4	1.814
8.804	5	2.840	1.101	5	22.730	0.176	5	141.748	11.023	5	2.268

To Convert	Multiply by
Inches to Centimetres	2.5400
Centimetres to Inches	0.3937
Feet to Metres	0.3048
Metres to Feet	3.2810
Yards to Metres	0.9144
Metres to Yards	1.0940
Miles to Kilometres	1.6090
Kilometres to Miles	0.6214
K'metres to Nautical Miles (U.K.)	0.5396
K'metres to Nautical Miles (Int.)	0.5399
Sq. Inches to Sq. Centimetres	6.4520
Sq. Centimetres to Sq. Inches	0.1550
Sq. Metres to Sq. Feet	10.7600
Sq. Feet to Sq. Metres	0.0929
Sq. Yards to Sq. Metres	0.8361
Sq. Metres to Sq. Yards	1.1960
Sq. Miles to Sq. Kilometres	2.5900
Sq. Kilometres to Sq. Miles	0.3861

To Convert	Multiply by
Acres to Hectares	0.4047
Hectares to Acres	2.4710
Cu. Inches to Cu. Centimetres	16.3900
Cu. Centimetres to Cu. Inches	0.0610
Cu. Feet to Cu. Metres	0.0283
Cu. Metres to Cu. Feet	35.3100
Cu. Yards to Cu. Metres	0.7646
Cu. Metres to Cu. Yards	1.3080
Cu. Inches to Litres	0.0163
Litres to Cu. Inches	61.0300
Gallons to Litres	4.5460
Litres to Gallons	0.2200
U.S. Pint to U.K. Pint	0.8327
U.S. Gall to U.K. Pint	6.6616
Cu. Metres to U.K. Galls	219.9690
Grains to Grams	0.0648

To Convert	Multiply by
Grams to Grains	15.4300
Ounces to Grams	28.3500
Grams to Ounces	0.0352
Pounds to Grams	453.6000
Grams to Pounds	0.0022
Pounds to Kilograms	0.4536
Kilograms to Pounds	2.2050
Tons to Kilograms	1016.0000
Kilograms to Tons	0.0009
Litres to U.S. Pints	2.1134
Litres to U.S. Galls	0.2642
Cu. Metres to U.S. Galls	264.1720
1 Barrel of oil to U.S. Gallons	42.0000
1 Barrel of oil to U.K. Gallons	34.9700
1 Barrel of oil to Cu. Metres	0.1590

International Paper Sizes

Size	Millimetres	Inches
A0	841 x 1189	33.1 x 46.8
A1	594 x 841	23.4 x 33.1
A2	420 x 594	16.5 x 23.4
A4	210 x 297	8.3 x 11.7
A5	148 x 210	5.8 x 8.3
A6	105 x 148	4.1 x 5.8
A7	74 x 105	2.9 x 4.1

Temperature

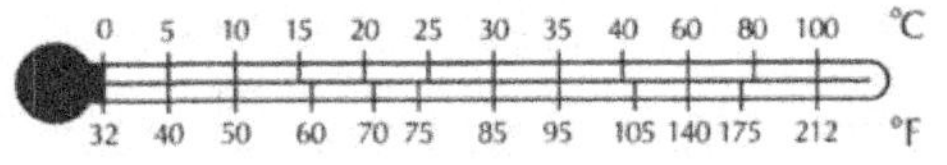

Speeds

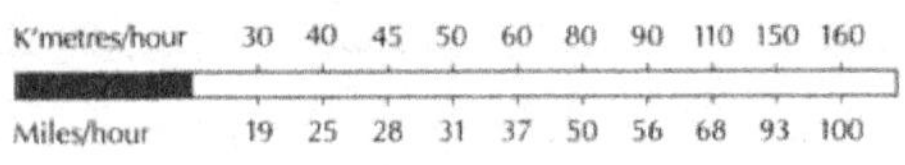

TIME ZONES + AREA CODES

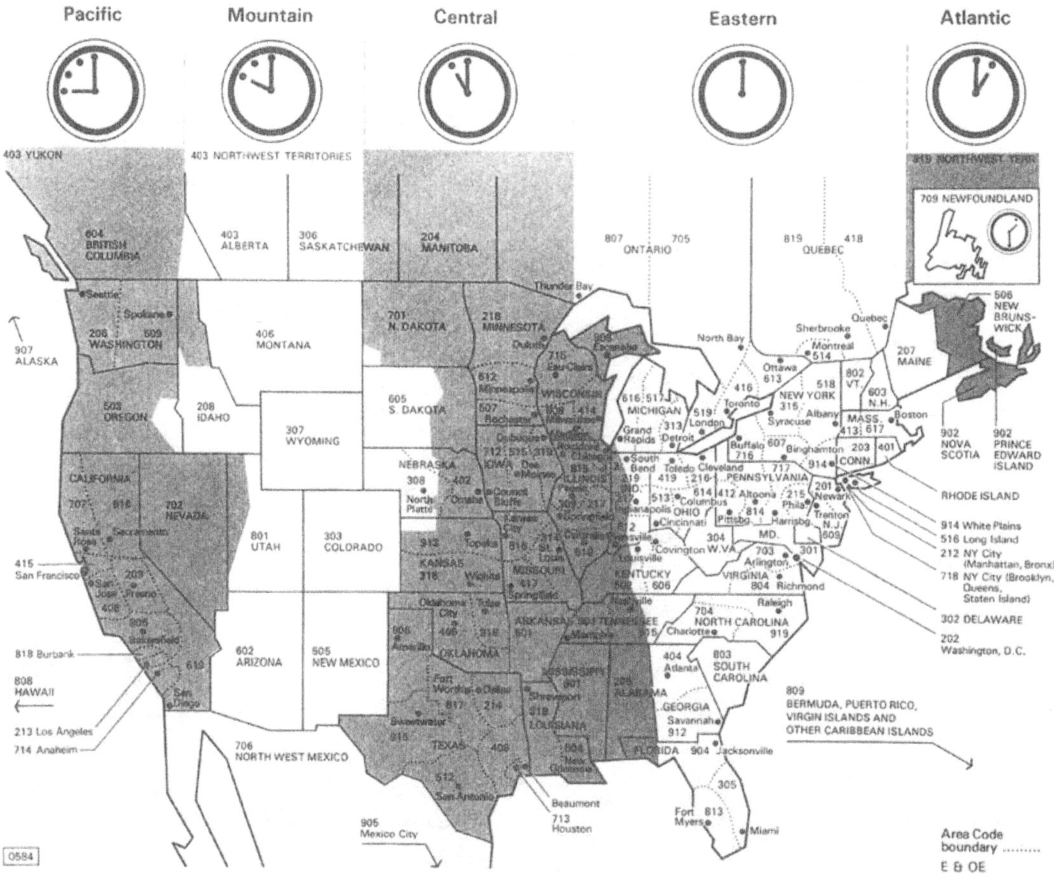

International Dialing-In Codes

To make an international call it is necessary to dial first the dialing-out code (011 in USA, 011 in Canada but 8011 in Montreal), then the dialing-in code followed by the subscriber number including the city code. For international dialing any first 0 or 9 should be omitted from the city code, except for France where the 15 or 16 only should be omitted. For the USA and Canada the full city code is dialed.

Argentina	54	Hong Kong	852	Netherlands	31	Singapore	65
Australia	61	India	91	New Zealand	64	South Africa	27
Belgium	32	Iraq	964	Nigeria	234	Spain	34
Brazil	55	Ireland	353	Norway	47	Sweden	46
Canada	1	Israel	972	Pakistan	92	Switzerland	41
Chile	56	Italy	39	Panama	507	Trinidad/Tobago	809
Denmark	45	Japan	81	Philippines	63	United Kingdom	44
Dominican Rep	809	Kuwait	965	Poland	48	USA	1
France	33	Luxembourg	352	Portugal	351	USSR	7
Germany (FR)	49	Malaysia	60	Romania	40	Venezuela	58
Greece	30	Mexico	52	Saudi Arabia	966	Yugoslavia	38

Standard Time Zones of the World

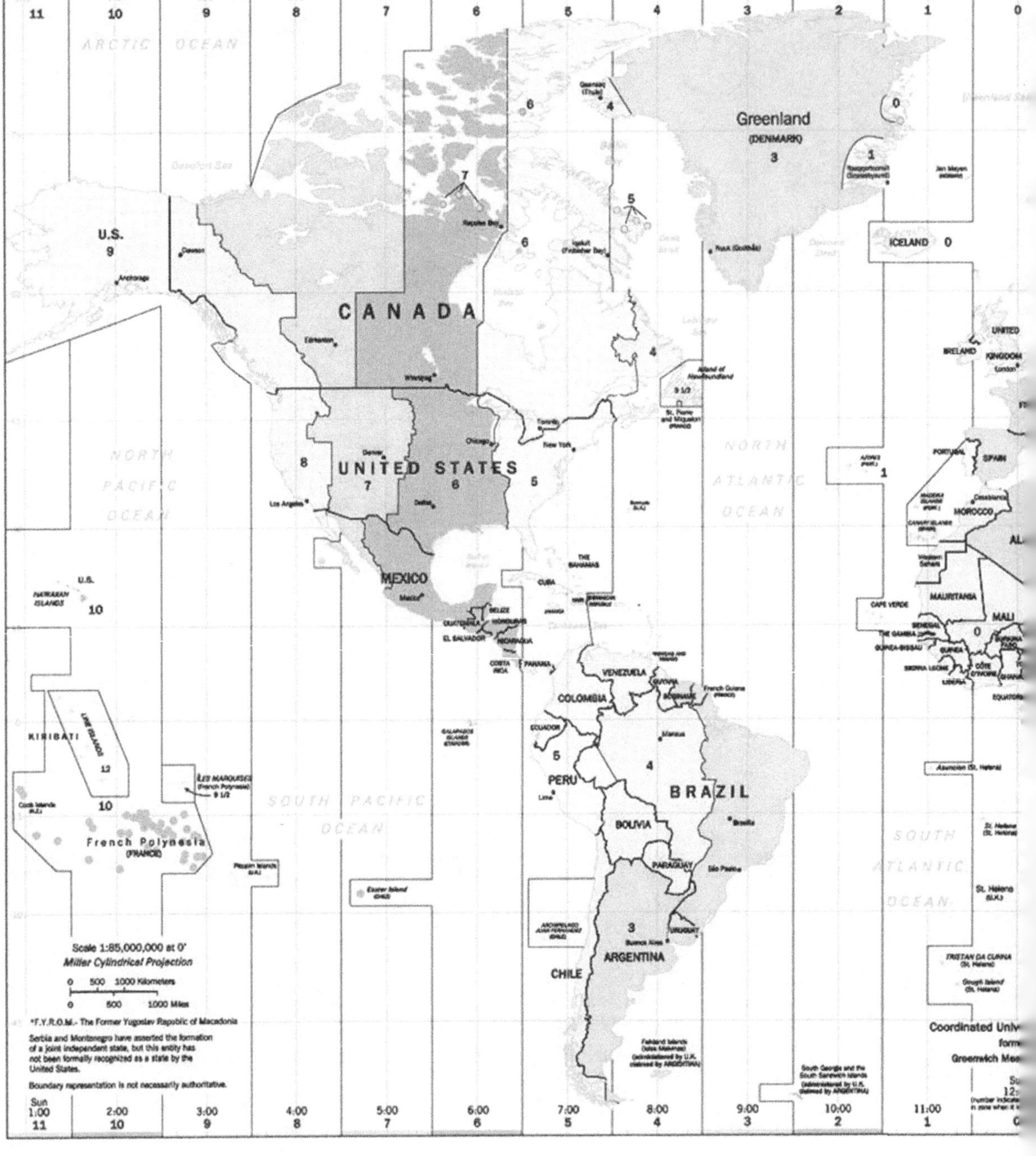

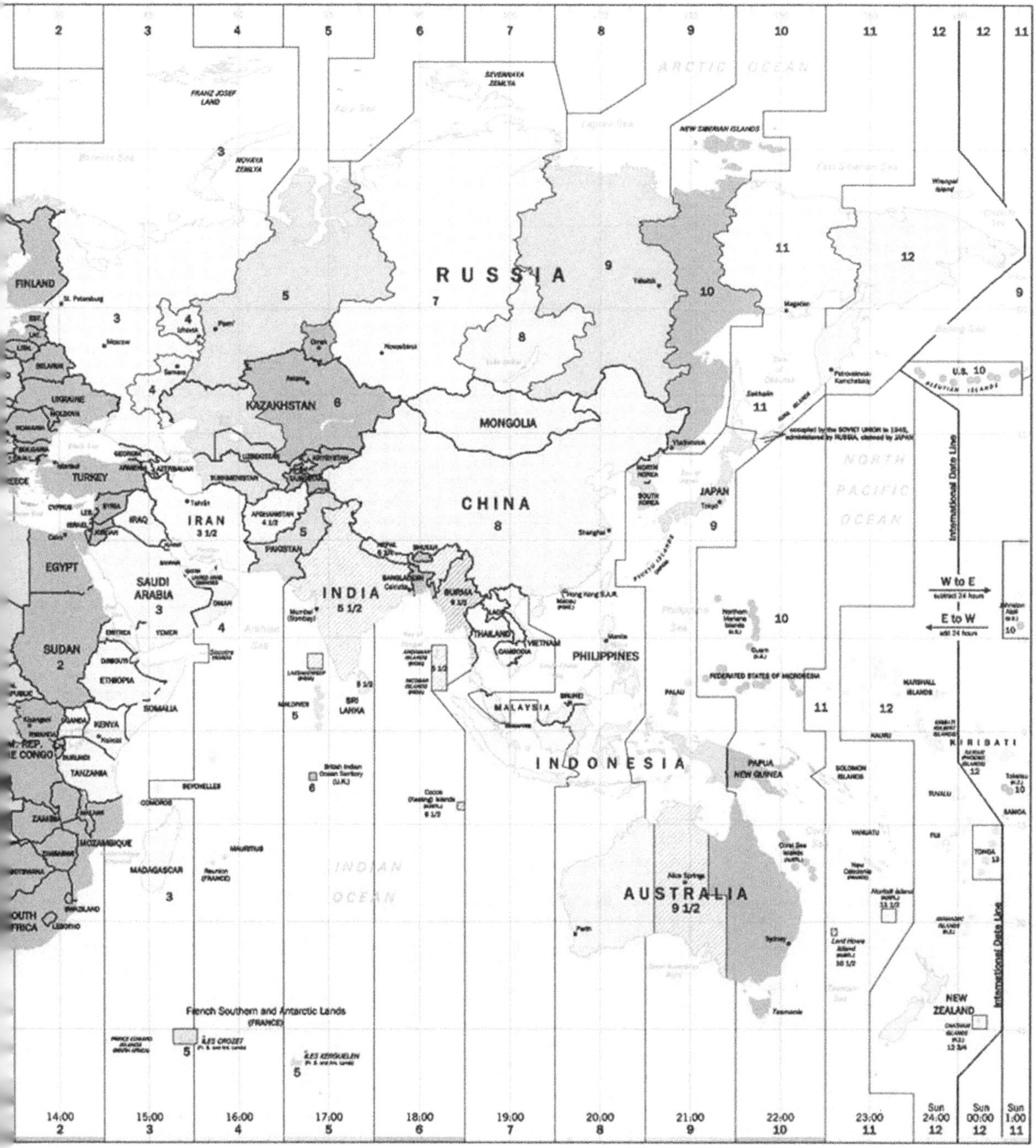

2
3
4
5
6
7
8
9
10
11
12
12
11
ARCTIC OCEAN
FRANZ JOSEF LAND
NOVAYA ZEMLYA
SEVERNAYA ZEMLYA
NEW SIBERIAN ISLANDS
FINLAND
RUSSIA
KAZAKHSTAN
MONGOLIA
CHINA
JAPAN
NORTH KOREA
SOUTH KOREA
TURKEY
IRAN
3 1/2
IRAQ
SYRIA
EGYPT
SAUDI ARABIA
SUDAN
ETHIOPIA
SOMALIA
KENYA
TANZANIA
MOZAMBIQUE
MADAGASCAR
SOUTH AFRICA
AFGHANISTAN
4 1/2
PAKISTAN
INDIA
5 1/2
SRI LANKA
BURMA
6 1/2
THAILAND
VIETNAM
CAMBODIA
PHILIPPINES
MALAYSIA
INDONESIA
PAPUA NEW GUINEA
AUSTRALIA
9 1/2
NEW ZEALAND
NORTH PACIFIC OCEAN
INDIAN OCEAN
KIRIBATI
TONGA
13
U.S. 10
International Date Line
W to E
subtract 24 hours
E to W
add 24 hours
French Southern and Antarctic Lands
(FRANCE)
ÎLES CROZET
ÎLES KERGUELEN
occupied by the SOVIET UNION in 1945, administered by RUSSIA, claimed by JAPAN
14:00
2
15:00
3
16:00
4
17:00
5
18:00
6
19:00
7
20:00
8
21:00
9
22:00
10
23:00
11
Sun 24:00
12
Sun 00:00
12
Sun 1:00
11

ADDRESSES

ORDER FORM

Order a 2014 Datebook for someone special in your life.
Remove this page gently from your datebook.
Fill out the form, include a U.S. Money Order, and mail it today.

** Order your 2015 Planner by November 1st and get it for $19.95!*

___	datebook(s) X $ 19.95 =	$______.00
1	packing, shipping, and signature required for delivery for 1 book	5.00
___	additional books at $19.95 each = (Example. 2 x 19.95 = $39.90)	______.00
___	packing, shipping, and delivery for each additional book ($3.00 ea.) +	______.00
	Total Cost	$______.00

* Please allow 4 -6 weeks for packing, shipping, delivery to U.S. Post Office, and postal delivery.

Examples.

The total cost for 1 planners plus packing, shipping, delivery = $19.95 + 5.00 = $24.95

The total cost for 2 planners plus packing, shipping, delivery = $39.90 + 8.00 = $47.90

The total cost for 3 planners plus packing, shipping, delivery = $59.85 + 11.00 = $70.85

The total cost for 4 planners plus packing, shipping, delivery = $79.80 + 14.00 = $93.80

Enclosed is a U.S. Postal Money Order for $______.00 for ___ book(s).
Send this form to: 670 Youngs Road, Suite D, Williamsville NY 14221 U.S.

Please ship the Planner(s) to:

Name ____

Address ____

City, State, Zip Code _____________________________

U.S. Phone & E-mail _____________________________

quarterboundpress.com